To Steve

ARRIVAL

Mary Barnet

Mary Barnet

Richard E. Schiff 2010

Illustrated by Richard E. Schiff

Published by Casa de Snapdragon Publishing LLC
A Traditional, Independent Publishing Company

Library of Congress Cataloging-in-Publication Data

Barnet, Mary Elizabeth.
 Arrival / Mary Barnet ; illustrated by Richard E. Schiff.
    p. cm.
 Poems.
 ISBN 978-0-9840530-8-7 (pbk.)
 I. Title.

 PS3552.A6958A89 2010
 811'.54--dc22

                          2010019830

20100523
Printed in the United States of America

ENERGY

Nor can energy envisioned,
The moment of revelation,
Or the sight of a creation die ;
For an eternal universe,
Past the crashings of the stars,
Can somehow be known in that thought.

THREAD OF LIFE

We pass the thread of life
From generation to generation
Offering up our souls to an indifferent eternity,
Constantly turning to look back
Then facing this hour
In a rededication of ourselves.

LAKE ON LAKE

I see you canoeing
Lake on lake
My sleep is sweet
Already I am in
The air about you
The dragonflies
That mate about you
Hold each other
With joy I was held by you
Our spirits frolic
Together ride the waters
Return to land
Bound in chains of pine and maple
I will always return
To look at your children
From time to time you will glance at mine
Love ensconced in frames of wood
Written upon the page
But, most of all, love eternally
Upon our breasts
Glowing forever

In the eyes of our joy !

7th Avenue Gallery

WHILE THE WATERS FLOW

Our way is clear.
Where ever we may go
Beyond, tomorrow is near.
As we are, love we know.
The Lord is with us here.
Though winter's winds may blow
On the vines of life,
We are like gourds,
Rattles shook in joy as well as strife ;
Worshipping Life with life,
Sunlight finds the spirit's ear
Trav'ling day and night with no fear…
The land we cross ;
Happy and safe, we roam the Sacred ;
We walk with the white-tail spotted deer !

Meeting

I might have seen you
As our subway cars passed between stops
Both of us looking out our windows.
I might have sat near you on the bus
Or stood over you as you read your book.
I don't know you when we see each other on the street.
Our paths may have crossed a thousand times,
Unless I saw you in the newspaper,
On TV or by some other chance.

Your face has a haunting familiarity ;
I won't forget you.

HAIKU ?

Dawn on a chill'd wooden porch
Tiny crescent within the crescent
Raccoon family footprints !

LIFE GOES PAST

Quickly, it seems,
Just as fast
As unremembered dreams,
Like temporary lodgings
Not properly cleaned.

There exists a glow
Beyond ordinary sight ;
By some hard-won Grace this beam
Can pierce the darkness with the light.

TO MY FATHER AT 76 – A TRIBUTE

Never stopping
Backwards to look
After spending the morning
Painting in your nook.

You walk for exercise and health.
Strength giving miles
Challenging the cold
And all its wiles.

Returning from your walk,
Six miles in the snow,
Over the icy sidewalk,
In your last years you go.

In the twilight,
Standing on the stairs ;
One sees strength –
Thinks not of armchairs.

Any man should be proud
Of a life that does not fade.
The strength to live long,
Wear well a life well-made.

TEARS

I see pain in your eyes.
Tears now are exquisite.
I need to sob now as do you.
To cry out
Is the joy of my pain.
Your storm nourishes me as welcome rain.

No Other thought

In an empty spare room of the mind
The wind brings stories I find ;
While I am in those wood far away
Hunger comes again to stay.
But you are in my heart
Even when we're far apart.
I asked then and I ask now
Think of me when no other thought you will allow

Mexico – The Day of the dead

Out of the sky
The butterflies descend
"The Day of the Dead" is here.
Time to celebrate the living
Candy skulls and chocolate tombstones
Our ancestors are dreaming of us.
And we, we dream of a future
that may never come.

CHILDREN

To be free
Cast off oneself
Return unhurried
To that world in which
Children dream.

THIS WORLD

This world not fit for man or beast
Whose lonely calling does not cease
When the touch of the hour is cold
Like a blanket it enfolds –
Flesh otherwise naked before the wind
Can be warmed in both soul and limb.
Our destinies tempered with wonder
On joyful moments our eyes alight :
Freedom signaled by the sound of thunder
Frees us not from earthly fright.

SOMETHING

Something has struck a beneficent cord in my heart
I bless the world he says and I,
I experience the bliss

of what is

my life

there are a thousand kinds of kisses
millions of songs
countless poems, written since the beginning
even dinosaur poems perhaps.

my breath in your presence is the deepest of kisses

Life, I love you too much.

Self Portrait   © Richard E. Schiff 2009

THERE IS GLORY IN THE MEADOWS

Gath'ring near the edges of the woods
With the power of their wisdom
The Elder women are meeting in council
Discussing War in The Longhouse
Because the Men have passed their message
The fate of the Tribe was up to them
They have gone to test their strength
On the Little Game the Whites have left them
For the meager dinner that remains
Prior to this war
Men & Women have decided together

Here we see the passing of The Tribes
Men go off to die
Women will starve or....
Make new husbands of the whites
Can we blame them ?
They were our great grandmothers !
They kept our blood alive !!!

ALL ARE ALIKE–WANT HAPPINESS

All the Same People who
Ate at my family table
Are here ---
All the people who
Sat at the first Thanksgiving Table
Are still here !..

I am trusting in God that we gather All Ways
Again for the Original Thanksgiving !
This Year !!!

TURNING, TURNING

Gargantuan tower
Wind driven mill of immense power
Like to the windmill home to Rembrandt in old age and
poverty
When Dutch New York flourished across the sea
Abundantly he painted
Full of talent but hardly considered sainted
Fallen from public grace
Still he held his place
For after his wealthy and beloved wife died
He took a lowly servant to be his bride
But yet in him his nation
And the world find cause for celebration
As from this place so full of life
Holding this land below the sea from flooding's strife
Pumper of waters hour by hour
Chief grinder of flour
Keeping back the North Sea
The windmill's arms turn and turn so that the screw can be
Savior and nourisher of its place of sovereignty
Of man and mill against the sea.

The Mill at Leyden © Richard E. Schiff 2008

MERCENARY SOLDIER

I've fought for other people's interests ;
I, a Cossack Jew hired
To fight for the Czar.
I ride at a moment's notice
Into a strange land
To live in homes that can never be mine
At war's end I ride home alone.
In exile these ten years
Carried from my last defeat
By a warrior wise and
Experienced in silence ;
I have found sanctuary at last.

I listen to the same song
Over and over
As if it were an anthem.
My cries are no longer oaths of battle :
My anthem echoes through the woods ;
Not words but the sounds of the
Love all about me.

The Willow in Winter   © **Richard E. Schiff** 2009

MIDST THE LIGHT

Absence nothing more than

Presence in the language of darkness

At the dance of light and life

All about us sunshine and growth

Growing from darkness and void

Yielded out dreams

Out that black trance

Life bears herself ---

In glory to the endless Creation

Glory, Hallelujah !

IN GHOSTLY TRIUMPH

The canine creatures run
Back and forth in yipping celebration ;
The smallest gath'ring around a
Half-filled pail,
Lapping up the afternoon.
The darkness creeps in with
Black-faced raccoon pups,
Their mother biting at the heels of night
Whose wildness replaces domesticated day.

SLEEP IS DANGLING

A modifier of consciousness
A calming of day's worries
Yet a bringer of fearful moments, too ;
Sometimes dreaming of waking nightmares
Only for the moment here
Free of the burdens of human thought and
circumstance.
In the vocabulary of today
Sleep brings tomorrow.

GASH IN THE SKY

Bloodletting gone awry
Gruesome songstress bleeding
Without a reason why
Only cutting the poem, cutting the flesh
Yanking the flower from the mesh
Out life's fabric the threads torn – wronged
To reveal a clotting reason
So that words are born, and like the burning
Desires of our humanity, cry out in song.

I KNOW THIS MOUNTAIN

As I know myself
I am friendly with the rain
The long fingers of the sun
Reach into the green and glowing forest of my mind
Fill my mind with strength
Give my muscles power
And fill my eyes with wonder.

AT THE MOMENT IS

Disappearing
We cannot get the drawer open ;
Until…
I can get this pen out,
Begin to write
Finish this thought :
Commend Time for including me ;
Rue the day I die
Though I only see it,
And forget my life forever.

BUS

An insect
Wasting his short life
Trying to pass through the glass.
Long antennae
Useless before the mighty monster
Of civilization.
Trying to help him
Might only crush his ting form –
A woman's laughter is familiar
As we wend our way through street after street.
This bus carries us all,
Doesn't it ?

BLIZZARD OF 2009

Dimly thru the falling snow
A long walk thru the fields
Icily shrouded
For a moment we think :
"It is surely unreachable."
But with our stronger nature
We know in our deepest place :
We will get there !

© Richard E. Schiff 2009

View From Our Front Door

NIGHT

Night has kissed my soul
So that
Cleansed at long last
I resolve to trust
the last friends
Welcome and serve the
lover and husband
I am slave too.

Death be not so proud
As to reject these bones
that ocean from which
We came
But perhaps I too
Shall bear a nation
By my death.

I WANT

I want to
To be
Someone of real importance
A figure of artistic speech
A sign of freedom
With the strength to rejuvenate in the sunshine of Faith
Always in the grasp of modern life.

I want to be
An exception(al)
To the rule
The person who is
Permitted to be
In the especial value
Of my art and my life
& my love.
I am this person
By the grace of God
It is life who gives me
All
That is of value.

GETTING THE BUSINESS

Biz-ness is Bigger
than Poetry
Can ever hope to be
But in the hour of rest
Sometimes a book
that guided our young lives
Re-emerges
Guides me through the dark hours
Into the dawn.

THE PULSING HEART

God is the pulsing heart of the universe
Expanding and contracting
Zillions of eons in time.

(IMAGINARY!?!) NEWSPAPER HEADLINE: MAN STEALS BREAD TRUCK

Police are investigating the theft, at 3 am in the
morning,
of a bread-truck from in front of a convenience store.
The perpetrator is being charged
with grand larceny, and "eating on the run,"
and faces 2-5 years in prison.
Justice follows crime:
theft caused by hunger brought on by poverty.
All for want of a mere loaf of bread ???

OVER

Over the mountains
The sunset hovers red
Red sun and crimson clouds
The sight condenses
To a moment of awe
Full of portent
Tomorrow the prediction
Of today's light
Fading to darkness
And night dressing at
The end of this glorious display
Crimson fades to black.

THINKING OF US

Sitting alone at night
After you are asleep
I think a thousand secrets
That cannot seem to keep

I remember in the silence
How you told me about yourself.
I think of what we said
And realize this burden is part of my wealth.

When yesterday looms in my thoughts
I push away what is not now.
I keep your secrets
Getting my sleep somehow.

In the morning when I wake
I see the sun.
I am living with your words
Thinking of us as one.

CORSICAN BROTHERS

Perhaps the golden stones
That rattle on the beaches
Have already grasped you
Passing in tomorrows' dreams
Perhaps in the glorious silence
Sacred feathers rattling
Within you the future has come
And like the wind you will
Disappear in a cacophony
Of precious stirrings
Walking the beaches of your love.

CLOVER

I am doing what I dreamed I'd do ;
I am making sweet love to you.

The hardest part has passed ;
Winter's gone at last.

In the fields the cold is over,
Blossoming into flowers and clover.

My time alone is ended ;
Our heavy coats are put away mended.

Both you and Spring time I hold dear,
After the cold has brought death so near.

We are born again :
You are my lover and my friend.

NOISE OF LIFE

It's long past here on this journey that I'm bound ;
Between this and there is many a winter's frost.
On these plains gophers and jack rabbits abound :
Night not silent but full with song.
In the chill winds now we're tossed ;
Beneath the earth, the noise of life
In their mounds of squeaking cacophony
The small creature with life is crowned.
Through the sky the planets cross,
The yellows, reds and blues of life astound
I wish to share the stark blue sky I have found.

SOMEWHERE

I.

Somewhere deep within
I could hear the cries of a drowning soul.
I remembered that
A part of us must die
To free the soul for growth.

II.

The day had gone well
But there was a feeling of dissatisfaction
As if something was lost or missing.
I sensed it.
I could not remember what it was.

III.

Do I know ?
Does anyone know
Toward the fulfillment of what dream,
On the path of what destination We travel ? Do you
know ?

THE SWIRL OF SUNSETS

One day after another
Beyond locations
Everywhere 5 O'clock
6:30 - purple people racing
With an orange sun
Across the night-near sky.

SHOPPING

I shop at the charity shop
Donations a dollar a piece
A room full of boxes of used garments
Take your pick
A man inquires about the food pantry
But they can't give you food unless
You register for food stamps
Come clean with all your sins of poverty
Your half-assed attempts at survival
You are guaranteed to be violating some law or another

By being poor.

Sheridan Square South   © Richard E. Schiff 2008

SUN

Thru the glass of the skylight
Lightly tripping along
Like a kindergartener skipping
In a race to maturity
Images before my hidden eye
Hold me fast to today
the wonder of the illumination
a book illustrated with reality
I, quiet and undisturbed
My home full of light reflected from that orb
that spins as if fanning away the heat of life
the blossoming of humanity
is silently running away from
the confrontation of my hours
In the youth of my eyes
all is vainglorious
Nothing alone survives age
so that in future we shall retrieve our cups
finding them full in a place crowded with clamoring
souls

if only we fill that decanter now
Never to stop their singing…
strong as the whales that call
one to another
the blackness of the void
is my eternal companion.
overcome yet with tongues full of words
to us the task to separate the dross
and give birth to the fulfillment of the moment.

DON'T LEAVE ME BEHIND

We sleep side by side
Yet in the morning
You say things I do not understand.

Don't leave me behind
Wait for me
Touch my limbs
As the wind touches the branches of a tree.

SNOW FALLS THIS JANUARY DAY

Looming deep within Martin's Day
America's new birthday
An unglamorous birth presages
Out of dark homelessness
A rededication of those empty,
              foreclosed homes
Not merely to former dwellers
But those long-lost hungry masses, as well
We cannot forget
One who waits empty-bellied –
Cold-shouldered by this nation......
Embrace me, and he, and she
All are in need, Take my
Hand , and his , and hers
All have something to give.....
I extend my hand &
Offer my embrace
My small gifts are yours to sup upon.....
Fill your heart !

GO SMILING

Go smiling
In that sweet night
The darkness is shrouded
Guides us above the rocks below
Crashing wave on wave
Guides us to where men gather
In small knots of greetings
Midst the Furies
Sweeping away our sadnesses
In a swell of changing lights
To crown the old with the new...
The impossible dream come true
A renewal
One who can play with fire yet not be scarred
At last it is real !

THE BROOKLYN BRIDGE

A fine bracelet
A jewel in the side of the river
Massive, yet delicate
Cables wider than a man is tall
Ferry where there is none
Making both sides one
Before it man is small
Its very existence on this earth is as a crown sits

I tried to walk across
But turned back
The distance was so great it made me shiver
Seeing the river far below beneath the cracks
On giant plates which the others crossed
Not me – I did not tarry on that bridge
But turned to the land and dreams of grass covered
ridges
More to my size
Though for man the span is the prize
Grander than the skyscrapers that nearby rise.

The Brooklyn Bridge

© Richard E. Schiff 2008

LONELY CREATION

We came and we heard
Sounds of a bird
Singing desperately
To save some words for posterity.

Children of another time,
Future students of the rhyme,
Can we speak to one another by this choice
And not let words passing smother our voice ?

You must know
Only in your eyes can my words grow.
I cherish the repetition
Of my otherwise lonely creation.

DECLARATION

Once I walked a different road.
You didn't stop for me when I was cold.
I couldn't travel far that way.
I didn't know it in those days.
You said I was lost,
Well that's another bridge I've crossed.
Now I've got to where I was going :
With each struggle I am growing.
Perhaps once more I'm heading on
Not knowing which foot to step first upon.
More certain in the greater things
I am ready for the fortune life brings.

TRY AND TRY AGAIN

You won't see me hanging out in bars no more
I'm not caught in that revolving door ;
Still I don't know where I am.
Sometimes my life doesn't seem worth a damn.
If I could speak this emptiness
To it you also would confess.
The truth is that we all are lost :
There are so many bridges to be crossed.
Every day we try and try again.
A foolish few resort to paper and pen,
Outcasts in the world of men
Who create some beauty now and then.

COMPLEMENTS AND COMPLAINTS

Some mumbled complaints.
Some complements –
Some dreamed of relief !
Desire without love
Is the same as camping at night
In the woods without a fire.

The hands might be anywhere on the clock.
It is all the same to me.
Death reached out
But lost her grip.
Almost immediately my friends
Back into their laughter slip.

ONLY FOR US

We stopped to look.

We saw the mountainside beneath the cold

Gray light of evening.

We heard the music of sparkling crystal on the air.

Life was warm then

Though she was not always fair.

We saw the grandeur of our imaginations

The glory of those colors which only for us were there

I HEARD (TRADITIONAL HAIKU)

The birds sing in Spring

At first light of dawn

The last hoot of the night-owl.

THERE

The sun falls hard on my back
The crow caws
Caws again & again
The rays beat
Beat on my scalp
My feet pad the earth
The earth is mine

May I rest there
There 'neath that tree
May it bear fruit
Fruit
That nourishes generations
Again & again...

OCEAN

I awoke alone
Like so many other days.
The tide rolled in
From beyond the bay.

I rose to walk the beach
Gazing at dying seaweed,
Washed by the waves,
From oceans' turmoil freed.

A storm beginning,
Clouds glower.
The wind pushes sand
Into the air with all its power.

The touch of a wave
Cold as the winds' reach ;
A chill seizing everything,
The swell pushes beyond this beach.

America on the High Seas   © Richard E. Schiff 2009

WITHIN
(CHILDREN'S HAIKU AFTER LEWIS CAROL & 'WINNIE THE POOH'):

I hear the squigg'ling
My tumkins squawks so
Frimsey is born thus in me.

ONE SUMMER EVENING AT THE BLOCK PARTY

As the small boys raced up & down the crowded
sidewalks
You put my four year old patent leather feet on your
shoes
And danced to the music of old Italian men
In the orchestra that
Serenaded the entire neighborhood
On our street closed off to the traffic
Under cast-off christmas lights.

PUSH THE HURT OUT

In my life of crowded solitude
My thoughts are a tired song.
Today is lost in imaginings of tomorrow.
Salvation I discover
When your bright arms I can no longer elude.
You hold my sorrow close,
Caress my brow,
Push the hurt out of now.

NEW WORLD AT LAST

A scar upon the land
Life is no trick
From Now on Take it or leave it !
It may be (y)our
Treat....!

BEHIND THE COLORED DOOR

In the silent world of dreams,
Beneath the staccato rap of the rain,
What land is this ?!!
Friends, lovers & enemies are a timeless stream ---
The sleep I am swimming in is a hurricane.

Peace is hard to find.
It cannot be bought.
We are lost in an eternity of troubles,
So that our minds are flooded and remind us
Of the ruin of that gilded dream we sought.

What we wanted no longer can be found.
Now we want more :
Some jewel from every land,
Each moment a different musical sound,
A gift behind each colored door.

Compromise is a lost art

Perhaps what we get is what we see.

Tomorrow blossoms when the season is right.

Sometimes what we taste of life is tart.

It is only silence that lasts forever.

YOU TELL ME

I retreat from life

I repeat for the hundredth time

I always have.

The two huge raccoons on the porch

Also retreat from light and danger

As I who have rarely

Conquered light and crowds

Also retreat into the quiet of

The two huge raccoons on the porch

HUMANITY

Great love I require
To know you
Sing my songs
Mouth my words
Love my worlds
Stand beside me always.
My struggle is yours
To hear the great sky
Rustling prayers
Within the green blood of the trees
Prayers that call to you
Making you warm within your lives
Cloaked in the wonder of my words
Full of the iridescent sea creatures
That swim in the skies of Time.

THREE HAIKUS

1

Horizon

One

Long Sun

2

Day

Wanes

Sun rises again & again

3

Night-fall

Sun setting

Here, and there

OVER THERE, OVER HERE

A dull
A dull, a dull
Throbbing of the sunlight
Thru the trees
The caw, caw, caw
Of the crows over there
Nearby
The pound..., pound..., pounding
Of the ocean on the lees
The glitter,
Glitter,
Glitter
Of the sand on the beaches
Over there
The spires
Reach,
Reach,
Reach to sky
As over here
In the throbbing of the sun

In the trees
The crows
Caw, caw, caw

COLD ROCK OF SOLITUDE

cold rock of solitude
clears the fields
dragged behind the horses
up & down hills
pushing the snow & ice
aside the trees
i am alone in the frost
winter of the soul
passing ever so slowly
by ; though she race
time drags me like
the cold rock
of solitude.

DEMISE

My inevitable demise
Will return me
To the flowers and the skies.
I will pass through that door ;
My soul dissolve in air ;
The colors of life exist no more.
I will be still
In the breath of the universal
Existence my molecules fill.
All will hold me yet
I will be
Always the soul you met
Yielding to the One
Eternity.

CENTRAL PARK

At the old Carousel ; Now gone ?
Haven't even seen the park in years.

But yesterday ! Oh, yesteryear !
How it shone and sang !
Its little jangling, singsong tune.

I rode the horse
And in the carriage, too.
Round and round, and sang
hummed its jingling tune
reached vainly in hopes of a ring
But there was none.

Then rode out over the fields,
past the children on line
And their parents waiting,
Gathered about that singular Merry-Go-Round.

© Richard E. Schiff 2008

Central Park

BEGINNINGS

They are erecting the red & white circus tent
On the old Wanamaker site
The aging vacation hall stands in disrepair nearby
The siding peeling to reveal
Gray shingles underneath
Like the tree nearby, standing a sapling then
Whose bark reveals the inner skin beneath.

ACROSS THIS LAKE

Life powers the engine of Time
with the souls of creatures
creating one & all.
We give birth
to our own daily breath.
We propel our existence
like a canoe
across this lake
whose branches and tiny leaves

also touch this water.

SUN

Glows red
Red birds circle
Over this clear space
Leafy trees
Are rising green
Into the greeting
Of a laughing sky

CONCEIVED IN RAINDROPS

Sprinkling the earth with life : meadows
Challenge that sun !
To bear these woods, like children
Spilling over the forest seems forever
Beneath the hand
Of an overbearing planets womb !

DANCE IN THE GLOW

In the glow of darkness
that is ours in the shining eyes of
love and friendship
within my land
that is everywhere OZ
I DANCE IN THE GLORY
in the world you've given me
I rattle the sun
in and out
so that I am born
again and again
free as the night
AND LOVING IT ALL

Artist's Mother   © Richard E. Schiff 2009

PAPA CROW'S FAMILY

The Crow family circles above
the grassy field, landing one by one
The small crowd of birds, having fun.
The largest caws slowly to his little band
gath'ring by the running waters of this creek
Where pine and hardwood grow out of the sand.
Clouds passing slowly do not block the sun,
Yet a thousand caws fill the afternoon :
Smoke from our little barbecue
Rises in a miniscule plume.
These fat birds circle as we eat ;
we finish but the crows go on
gathered cawing on the grassy knoll
from trees they're perched ; they depart
as the thunder of an eve'ning shower
through the air is rolling.
Likewise we race home
To rest in dry homes
While the rains fall.

SUNRISE

the night explodes
Giant fingers of light :
the hands of creation
hold me in the cradle of night
born again with each day
Darkness, prisoner carried
into these hours of glory
so that I glow---life tingles on my skin
in the power of this beautiful rainbow
from Time's spread-eagle prism.

THE RIDE

1.

The slender woman
Took the seat I offered her
As older than I - perhaps in her seventies.
A tiny woman
Whose identity otherwise
I could not scan.
She had been robbed of "everything"
Twice in her life
Never to achieve the goal of her youth
To study piano at Julliard.
She boarded the bus south
Commenting, "I think I'll like it down there."
Her destination, much less
Any return to a possible home, doubtful
But that importance lost
In her enjoyment of the ride.

2.

The driver's radio announced
A bus stopped by the road ;
Soon another group of passengers
Boarded the roaring creature
Of the spinning wheel we rode.
They found a place, each one
And I had to cease pointing out landmarks
To share my seat with a weary woman
Returning the long way
Home from her work
Glad to be ever nearer that place
To rest for the night
Before finding her way to tomorrow again.

THAT WHICH IS ALL

Climb the mountain
Swim the sea
Walk thru the door
Into eternity
Share Time with,
Dance with the Creator
Endlessly
For He is you
And you are She
Open your arms wide
To every life you abide
With the Creator always
A part of that which is
All

THERE IS

there is poetry
in the words we speak
we hear valleys
& mountains ride the earth
where sparkling dinners are eaten of sun-
birds dancing in costumes of glowing leaves
hot with the tune
that love gives to us
Life
and the living of it !

LET THE MORNING CARESS ME WARM

as a pool of water from which I'm born
let the eve bear my body to the earth
seal my life for what it's worth
cleanse me of
my failings so bold
now that youth is past and I've grown old
let me live in this suspended Time
where today is
the total of my birth

REQUIEM

There's a long finger pointing
To the edge of the world.
There's someone anointing
Near where the waters whirl ;
Spinning waters suck us in,
Spit us out,
Give our head a trim.
Like a washing machine
Mix our dreams
In and out : inside out.
Spin us all about.
Cannot we open
The little box
Wherein the Christ-figure resides ?
Can we not free our very souls
From the whirling waters
Our soul embroils.
Until she finish us and
Spit us out ?
Cleansed ?

DAY

Calculate the length
of days seemingly forever
stretching past the clothesline
in the sun on the lawn
minds travel through trees,
sparkling !
where creatures play,
through octagonal windows :
rainbows everywhere
real as eternity.
cut short only by the duration
of our eyes extending
through every breathing creature.
beyond the axis
earth spinning in the sunshine :
the everywhere
that is space and time,
In the memories of man
eternally recorded : sparkling !
brilliantly sparkling of now

experience holds forever in our arms
this revolving day, and night, and day...

GIANT ORANGE FISH ON THE LAWN

Out the window
Out the tank where six
Huge "gold" fish is become
Five, though our wealth is not
Greatly diminished.

THE AFTERHOURS

When women of the night
slink "home" with men
who do not know their names :
mornings that are still
wet with hangover headaches,
forgotten cooing
that knows not any
day that follows not-love
whirling skirts, dancing hips and double drinks
gone with the dawn.

GOD'S HANDS

Always beginning
Now passing midpoint
In this human race
A journey whose end we try not to think of
Whose rhyme and meaning
Are in reality the only
Possible and noble completion.
For even if we die alone
Happy or humiliated
Saved or lost
This and only this ending
Completes the tune God has played
Weaving our lives into the fabric of this world.

WHEN VISIONS BLOOM IN THE NIGHT

Dawn tells us secrets
Planets whirring in black universes
Reveal what we cannot know
Nothing is lost in a complete
Understanding of a meteoric
Trail of Brightness and Life.

SMALL EMERGENCIES

I was tired and cranky
Playing with the band
I held my rattle again
Shook it softly, but it fell ;
With my rendition of small disasters
My sweet niece smiled ; we laughed
At these stories, again I had to tell.

IN TRUTH

the value of each day
with us carries a fortification
castles of thought
guard us from our fear
vast spaces so near
the darkness of forgetfulness
passing to empty space.

ABSENCE

is only
another word
for a different color of the night...

MAGICAL WORLD

This world has slapped me silly.
With God's grace,
Nothing can hurt me again
I wander in the garden
scrawling messages to the sky
Brothers, forgive us
Even as we trans grace
Into the womb of Time
Perhaps, All is at last opalescent and pure
In your arms.

WORLD

We walk through this world of governments
There is no place to escape to
We must retreat into the forests
The joy of our minds will blossom in time
Doors will open relative to the bliss we find
The love and succor we give
Perhaps will reflect a good light

SWEET LITTLE SISTER, EARTH

Your big brother, Mankind
With his laws, his money
Almost destroyed you
With his poison
But now it is his land
That is a prison.
You are still singing :
Chanting the name of God :
In the Garden no one can blaspheme.

THE KEY IS PATIENCE

Joy excruciatingly beautiful
The worldly days,
Populated by the curious ;
Crowned by the blind wondering of eventualities.
Boyish, sometimes churlish
Pups whose wildness buds
& snails then in play
While we here remain,
Servants of the Great Spirit.

GLAD ARRIVAL

I am feeling smilier than ever ;
Chipmunks race back & forth in the driveway,
Scattering like russet leaves
Dancing to glad music
As your car is approaching.

UNTITLED #5

this place
another world seen bare
from the road of so many worlds
among which I sit
and where I am
worldless.

THE SUN IS RISING ON ME

Alone in a bed
In Mexico City my illusion of security has disappeared
There is only the light entering the tiny window –
Perhaps this is from a street lamp –
I close my eyes and it does not matter.

SONG

Choppy dream
Lake notes
The white tops
Cresting in the storm
All around
Tiny as our imaginings
Great as the anthill
By the shore
That is doused
City of the small
World where a millisecond is an eon.
A flashing neon light
Drowning in the panoply
Of light that is a city ;
All our creations
Out ! With the overload
Our grandiose scheme
Ended with a miscalculation
And we only
Unworthy gods

Inhabiting a darkness
That only need forget us
And we are gone
Buried in a wave of black creation
The void returned.

LESS

Could I be windless
In a windy time
In a windy city
A country girl
Alone when others'
Lives are crowdy.
I'm an old lady
Who wants to settle down ? An old lady ?
"Look ! It's true
She wears old lady shoes…"

THE SOUL CALLS

She cannot speak
The beauty or the squalor
within.

She cannot touch
The light and the darkness
without.

There is a small sound
As if a plant were to
Reach up.

The old answers are no good
The soul calls
For food.

LEGACY

In the company of strangers,
Lost in my home,
Repeating the words
Until all meaning is gone,
Such is my legacy

I speak frankly
Of the dishonesty of crowds.
This voice is my answer
To a world I do not understand
Whose reply to me is no reply at all

THE LAST OLD TOM CAT

The last old tom-cat---
The one you daren't spay---
His age made him delicate.
He was set in his ways.

White in color as in age
Pushed out of the kitchen and his meal.
The Exterminator came today
On his poison can he broke the seal.

The dog old too :
Dirty and sick ;
Confined to basement and yard.
The house only for cats to sit by chimney bricks.

Lying prone
In sleep as in death ;
The same life as mine
Gives you, my lovely pet, your breath.

FRAGMENT

What I have learned from Youth
The most important thing perhaps :
To have a sense of humor
Be able to laugh at yourself
and realize that life is sometimes
A continuous practical joke
Is my own sense of It.

CENTER

In the center
of the great dancing cosmos
the light of turning life
The squirrels arguing on the lawn
over a seed
the Acanthus, Jersey pine
All around
the grasses grow every minute.

THE ESCARPMENT

The greatest of the gods of the Catskills
Points a finger – stone flies to clear the path
As with a talon
With jagged precision a cliff is cut :
The river bed to the Hudson
Feeding the trees that hug the escarpment.

Below in Interstate Park
Families play and eat ;
We are crossing the Washington Bridge
See the people small in the distance

Imagining the stories of those
Who bragged as youngsters
They'd sat on the cliff they'd climbed
Just part way up in the trees
But safe from discovery for truancy.

Escarpment – The Jersey Palisades   © Richard E. Schiff 2008

IN THE DARK MINGLED

Glory of afternoon
Lavender cattails
Grow from the railroad
Up to the turnpike
Beyond these tracks that once bent forever
Into the wind beyond today
Bridges laced in steel
Are huge bracelets crossing the marshland
For small men whose dreams are larger than
The stunning simple beauty
Of small birds and furry mammals.

TOM CAT

Into heaven
Where the old Tomcat resides
A great immutable eye
And I, I in my new life
Touched by joy
Midst the fruits of eternity
Touching the nervous system
Touching the life wiring of this universe
On a glittering, glistening web
The dew is gathered to link the stars.
I, I read my e-mail at home in Orion
Where each day we eat donuts
Yet stay as young and thin
As we wish, we are.

AFTER BRAQUE

Grandpa's broken alarm clocks
On the table all in a clutter ;
After the fire,
Long after he and Nana passed.

Internet bill in readiness there for us,
Next to that for the plots we are paying off at the
cemetery.
While Mom, past 90, is 6 months and more on her
feeding tube.

So that we have come early to this beautiful Lords' park
Because we are fatigued.

I AM TRAVELING

In my mind
Far away from today
the moon rises over the beach
And the palm fronds
Rustle in the night breezes.

THE DULL

the dull, the dull, the dull
pounding of my heart in my ears
repetitive sound of the days
leaking out their existence
from the spent purse
that is my life

TO MY DEAR COMMANDER

Lost in Outer Space
Special Delivery Air Mail
Highest Commendation for D.S.
"Fleet of Foot & Loyal to Family & Nation"
Always Best in Our Eyes
The Chimney Swallow hiding mornings
Sings where the *mystic woman* 'mad with G-D'
chants in warbling words ---
The Bird Woman herself calls angrily to G-D :
"why ! why ! why !"

I call, in reply :
"Return ! Return !
Please ! Return !

FRIEND OR LOVER

Death is not my friend.

Yet always I await her arrival :

A lover who whispers sweet nothings in my ear.

Consuming like fire,

Leaving the ashes of time passed.

She takes one after another,

Friend and foe alike.

She lies with us

A frail lover more permanent than lover or wife.

She courts every man.

We struggle with life's passions in her arms

Until finally we are weary and welcome sleep.

CATS AND CATS

Lincoln Tunnel
Sped you & I
UK open top roadster
Home 'til you came
Lady & Baroness
The 'Rolls' to the core
destination <u>Vanguard</u>
Greenwich Village

Where Thalonious Jazzman
swung from the chandelier
Now from night air, jazz is emergent
We three, your convertible
off to *Washington Heights-*
In his home Thalonious dreams

No longer discordant
Walking in sleep
He sings to my no
"Have you heard me play ?"
Thalonious at his Grand

I meet the man of Jazz !
"Have you heard me play ?"
I admit to no
The beautiful piano he plays for me !

I return with Nica
to her house on *Weehawken* cliff
She says her "Cats & cats !"

MAY DAY 2007

Out of the corner of my eyes
I caught the first purple
Blood blossom of the Azalea
I knew the spring...
Morn had begun to bloom
Budding, the new year was before me

BLUE WORDS

red song
woman's words : what's gone wrong
till she cries out
in song and deed
join me to
the man as seed
let me walk among the throng
never from my womanhood freed.

I HAVE MY OWN DREAM

Every Thanksgiving
I hope to see alive and free
Feasting on this joyous Life
The children Solomon could not save.

Only in that way
Does humankind put an end
To a world of war.

WINTER

The wind rattles the windows ;
Cold seeps under the sill.
Somewhere in the woods tonight
The wanders a doe
Whom withered grass will not fill.

Mary Barnet

ALONE ON THE DUNES

that cold summer's night
moved away from the "dune party"
noisy kinds throwing beer cans
I moved away from their retching
to the crest of 'Blueberry Hill'

There slept in my wool Plaid
lined black cape Like a tent
yet exposed to all the elements of life
alone with the sky
And the eternal call
of that wild place & TIME.....

Kitty Genovese © Richard E. Schiff 2009

WINDING THE HIGHWAY

through racist 1960's Mississippi
And I, fifteen
alone with my black 'old man' ;

Ready to be strung up
If caught with this white girl
Thru Ol' Miss
toward Brownville,
Texas and beyond.
Along curling mountain roads
rife with Indian men and women
tending the steepest slopes of corn rows,
Towards the hungry streets of Mexico City
Where, almost homeless
we eat day old rolls
and wander those streets
Past the huge white Russian Embassy
The little Cuban consulate
with the miniature deer in the courtyard
In search of some greater fortune.

BREAD LINE

The Woman child
standing on line
at the food pantry
Gulping
Choking ever so slowly on her poverty...

GREAT BRIGHT EXPLOSION

Rumbling in the darkness
Morning flashes into our midst
Consuming the night
In flaming sunlight
Births the singing of the birds
Purple & pink
The horizon stretches
Everywhere !

AS WE WERE, WE ARE

I.

In the softest place
Behind your ear
I see us as we once were
Myself as I might have been
If not trapped in hallways where I found
In the land of melancholy & elation
Delusions lurking
Until I was guided from the recesses
Into a gentler life.

II.

I find retirement
After a lifetime of work
Service, art, & suffering
In a world of Peace & contentment.

III.

The alter gives me
Where she stole "once"
She returns "now" to me
I am green as apple jelly
In my old age free
From the weight of worry.

IV.

All's well and so
Seems awhile
I rest easy...

V.

I SMILE
SMILE A SMILE OF RELIEF !

UNTITLED #33

Before the Cosmos
To the sound of flutes
Once we danced ;
Before the altar of our lives
We stood entranced.

I must go far away
From the droning whirr and city noise
Worrying about tomorrow and today
And that constant hurry that so annoys.

I want to hear the flutes again
To hold each day close
Rise singing in the morning
Stand naked before the cosmos.

COSMIC STRIPPER

We strip away
Those vainglorious hours of youth
Until naked
Old age, like infancy
Cloaks us in the truth of Time
Escaping into the cosmos
A flame of consciousness
Billowing into a cloudless
Pristine sky
Clean in the one first burst
Light sleeping in infinite consciousness of forever..

SMILING

Go smiling
In that sweet night
The darkness is shrouded
Guides us above the rocks below
Crashing wave on wave
Guides us to where men gather
In small knots of greetings
Midst the Furies
Sweeping away our sadnesses
In a swell of changing lights
To crown the old with the new...
The impossible dream come true
A renewal
One who can play with fire yet not be scarred
At last it is real !

A WAY FOR US TO BE

Come with me
Touch the day
Awaken morning
With the song of the birds
Hold my hand and walk with me
Out of doors where the crickets chirp
And evening turns to glorious night
Look what they are doing
Bearing children
Building bridges
Caressing one another
So let us wend our way
Into a new world
A brave and new place
A special chapter for you and I...
A way for us to be.

TOMB OF THE UNKNOWNS

The soldiers march 21 steps
Pause 21 seconds
Death is not the final reckoning
The Unknowns' glory is beckoning
From stony depths
Found in his loss
He cannot be freed of battles' cross.

His guardians lead most exemplary lives
No alcohol passes their lips
Pure is the essence they are sipping
Into cussing and useless argument they are never
slipping
From good conscience only, they strive
To live without honor's loss
Never from their duties' roster their names out-cross't.

Those whose burial heard 21 guns
These names have they memorized
The honor of these soldiers realizing
Their nation's finest memorializing
As they, and those they guard are goodly sons
To bear their nation's triumphs' loss
As did all American heroes
Buried beneath six-pointed star, crescent , or cross.

BASH BISH FALLS

The water cascades
As over the shoulder a woman's braids
to a crystal, almost bottomless pool
Far from the world's mechanized tools
Here all the creatures have always drank
So for the lush growth we give thanks
Water clean as a fresh bathed babe
Colors that never fade
Oh bountiful water
Though elsewhere you may falter
Here you are abundant as the sun
Source of mankind's you, life, and fun.

Bish Bash Falls © Richard E. Schiff 2009

BEHEMOTH

A ship far out at sea
Is a lonely place but free
Mankind is meek before this roll of his dwarfed ship
In the roll and swell his wings are clipped
Yes, the gargantuan water
Mocking the sailors tiny quarters
So that no matter how mechanized
Her force the greatest giant can paralyze
The bird before its grandeur is small as a speck
Only hard work and grace prevent a wreck
The ocean is lonely
Not a vision of joy only
For here man's choice is freedom
The coiling waves leave us powerless to out-speed
them
We are miniscule before the soul
Of the waters that like a kettle boil.

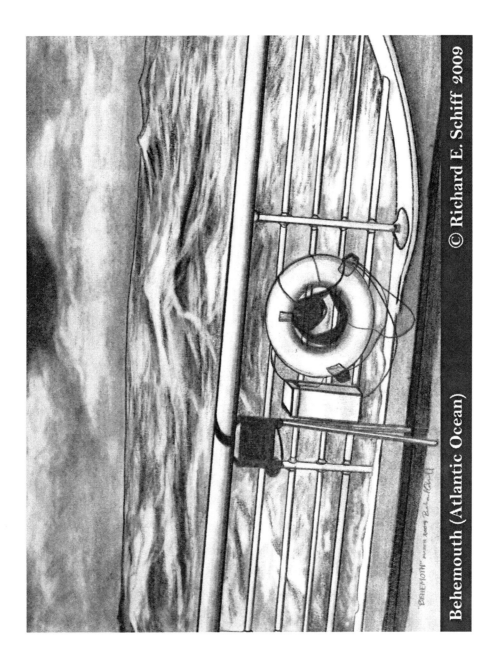

Behemouth (Atlantic Ocean)   © Richard E. Schiff 2009

UNTITLED #44

Might have
Might have been
Is
Is already
Will you ever set me free ?
Happy contented laugh – *nice* chuckle
Guess what ?
I am free already
Have always been
And – sometimes I believe
- in my dreams I know –
It will continue forever
The joy of seeing what I create
Knowing I can speak to God
Because He has set me free
I know I am
He speaks to me again
As He always has
Because I know
It is He who tells me what to write

I am God's creation

As is every living creature

On this our first eternal world

On the lakes and in the woods

Where men and women really should be

We really are

Free to share the joy of being

God's creatures.

GREENWICH VILLAGE BACKYARD

Out the backdoor or simply from one's window perch
The wooded corners still exist
We try to cover each and every crack with cement
Keep the earth covered
But here there are trees and bushes
A courtyard or an abandoned corner
of this miraculous earth.

What poet ? – Did Edna St. Vincent Millay muse
here ?...
Or did Tom Paine sit under this tree ?…
Did Washington walk here ?...
Did a lord kiss his lady ?...
Or a scullery mad hug her paramour ?...
Did men work hard indoors and come outside to rest a
moment in the sun ?...
To mark whose property was that fence nailed to that
tree ?...
Who owns this tree ?...

Dare I venture here ?

Backyard Greenwich Village © Richard E. Schiff 2009

Mary Barnet

THE BABE & THE BOY

To a hospital bed now confined
By a horseback fall seemingly doomed to lay
Only someday, to walk on crutches
Hardly wanting to see the day.
He says, " Only one thing will cheer me up :
A baseball signed by the Babe will !"
From the whole Yankees team with names combined
Comes the dedication for all to see
For on the ball he clutches
The Babe has underlined
"I'll knock a homer for you in Wednesday's game"
So that by the radio on the table
Sits a boy once doomed to be lame
But sure enough the Babe knocks one out
(These things happen when Babe is about)
For the boy : fate will soon make him well
With a singular ball, and a tale to tell.

© Richard E. Schiff 2009

Home Run

A GLOWING CONCEPTION

As in the eye of an insect
Large as a wail
The formation of humankind
Is huge before the tale of the tiny
Grand in the scheme of today & tomorrow
The human organism lives.

I bleed the words from myself
Hard as the surface between pen & paper
I am alone within the shell of my skin
One giant piece of joy
As green as the grand moss
Over the earth the gel of life singing
The dark bursting
Into the light born
Again a mountain of beings
Decorated with love
A glowing conception.

RED, YELLOW, AND GREEN

Mid your red sleep at dawn
A flower bursts :
The rose, red with spring,
Blossoms while the dew is eaten by a hungry sun.

Light has already waked the depths – there sun seethes ;
Rays fall slanting
The yellow streams straight
Soaking growth green into life.

TEARS

I see pain in your eyes
Tears now are exquisite ---
I need to sob as others do.
To cry out and reach for you
Is the joy of my pain.
Your storm nourishes me as welcome rain

EVERYWHERE

High waves grow higher
Against a darkening black.
Wave meets void
Yet does not bind.

that moment
Where touch and change occur
Is a flower
Blooming in a breathing sea.

LONG DISTANCE BUS

Bus line in the Port Authority Terminal
Chinese woman, and child ;
Two Haitian women ;
Two elderly white women ;
A Native American man.

I send my old Mom
To visit in Massachusetts.

One by one, a woman asks a neighbor
To watch her bags, until
The Native American looks at me
Pointing to his things.
I am touched that my friend has picked me out.
He will guard my Mom.
I bid her, "Say hello to our ancestors."
And he, he nods
In understanding of a place
We all come from.

Mary Barnet

RETURNING ON THE BUS

Another vacation over.
Another holiday gone.
Another bus to take.
Again I return alone.

Soon today will be
But a memory ;
This moment passes
So quickly into eternity.

Some say there is a plan.
I wait for some arrival.
Meanwhile, I plot and plan
Another month of my survival.

I hope some day to pause,
Turn and see your face,
Stop and see the place
Where past and future interlace.

There are times
I cannot write or rhyme –
When this confrontation
Does not yield a line.

I wonder what it matters
That I sit alone.
Another hour passes.
I am returning home.

BEGGAR'S BOWL

It is the same tale
Told a thousand times
That holds the beggar's bowl,
Gives the boats their sail,
And blesses me with rhymes.

MOTIONLESS IN NIGHT'S WOMB

I cannot comprehend death.
The thought takes away my breath.
To disappear in a shower of sparks
Or see a body preserved without marks
Is more real to me
Than any abstract measure of eternity,
I lie motionless,
A thousand years in darkness
Like a mummy in his tomb,
A dead body in night's womb
Until the record of these pages
Is the burning end of time ---
End to any human rhyme.

WRATH

I draw a warm bath
To escape the winter's wrath.

At the risk of being crude
I will not describe myself in the nude.

Age is not at all kind
I leave in silence what I find.

Suffice it to say I sit in the tub
As off me the day's grime I rub.

Even half an hour's shower
Hasn't got enough cleaning power.

Only with diligence can I be cleaned of the grime
Collecting since the beginning of time !

Mary Barnet

FROM MOM

Know that I am there
With you now
& only time and space
Keep me from serving you eggs
On that worn-out counter.
You are tomorrow ;
I am the world all about you.
And though I sleep now
I am with you always.

Awaken with me !
For I am the sun in your eyes !

Sometimes the sorrow is so sweet
It is joy as darkness sweeps over
The mountains that will awaken again
At dawn that casts our work
As a shadow of our lives
And our love as the skeleton
Upon which we have grown to old age.

© Richard E. Schiff 2009

7th Avenue Gallery

BLIZZARD BOUND

Rescued in the nick of time
By youth grown old.
You are at the door
I say, "Can you help ?
"Yes I'll get a friend."
Another nephew arrives
We leave
Free at last
Old age lets us go
For a minute
We are young
Of death, in our hearts, we are free.

Winter Park Scene

SNOW NIGHT IN THE PARK

© Richard E. Schiff 2010

STURM UND DRANG

Lightening & deafening explosions
Firecrackers & bombs
What other evil lies before us ?
Can we not dwell in the land of dreams
Ever again ?

No Where to go
That is not a frustration of this day ?
The shining light of creation
Drowned in a reality of starvation and illness.

What can we do
But grasp the soft flesh
Of light that tries to flee ?

We must dance in the darkness !

OUR ELEMENT

We walked the halls
Of the Metropolitan
You with your pain
I with my cane
Scoured the museum
Joyfully sampling hundreds of Masters.
In our element
Overcoming our impediments
Every segment was ours alone
Ignorant of the crowds were we :
Every room was ours
We were the artists' dream companions
Their beauties we did see
Their trials were our own.

Here we found etched in eternity
Growing in joy
Our very own story.

ONE MORE POEM

If I can only
Wring one more poem
From these lips ;
If only in this world my sewing
Could heal a torn muscle,
Or stop this ship's sails from blowing.

I have heard the music ;
Without those tunes
I have nothing.
It is a secret written in Babylonian runes,
Undecipherable and enigmatic
As the song a cricket croons.

Yearning for completion
Reaching beyond our powers
Seeking a final destination,
We are distant from the crowds :
As free as the medieval man,
Or a prince confined in a tower.

CHRISTENING

The silence is a beautiful song,
A christening of this inner self :
A child otherwise ultimately alone –
This creature of feeling
With each word emerges reborn
She lives anywhere in the universe
Both morning and moon are her home.

DENY DEATH

I am building a world
Where destruction
Once breathed a murderous breath.
Let us break free
Without destruction
Let us plant a new life like a tree.

LOOSELY

like liquid garments
floating free
in an in determinant place
that is me
that is all
that exists
nothing is all that is real
my hour is come
here I am, Death
naked in time
swimming before your eyes
in the milk of my life
suspended and free
in the space of this hour
the song of this minute
the voice of this moment
IS, my jewel.

INDEX

ABOUT MARY BARNET

Mary Barnet's first book, *The New American/Selected Poems* followed four chapbooks, including *Orchidia* and *Landscape*. She was the Featured Writer in a special edition of *Poet Magazine*. Her poetry has appeared in *Crossroads, Gusto, New Worlds Unlimited, The New Jersey Poetry Society Anthology, Funky Dog Publishing, Recursive Angel, The Greenwich Village Gazette, The Poem Factory, Numbat, The Pittsburgh Review,* and elsewhere. Mary has read in Judson Church and Grace Church, The Baggot Inn and the Figaro Cafe, all in Greenwich Village, and the Avanti Gallery in Manhattan, as well as with the "Saturday Afternoon Poets" at libraries in New Jersey. She read at and directed a Seminar at a New Jersey Poetry Society Convention.

She is founder and chief editor of *PoetryMagazine.com* and produces poetry films with Richard E. Schiff.

Mary's work has been reviewed by Adam Donaldson Powell who has stated that "many of these poems are carefully tailored pearls that could only have been written by a mature artist." Janet Brennan calls her work "intelligent and stunning poetry." She comments that her poetry "weaves her own images of her beautiful homeland into her poetry as only a lover of life can do" and says her work conveys the "values that our country was founded upon." Grace Cavalieri has said she "is a light to poets and the world..."

Dr. Krishna Srinivas from *International Poets* says of her work that there "is an underlying honesty and integrity of language, of emotion, of form in her poetry. She has a natural feel for language. Her expression is lucid, facile and spontaneous." Prof. Syed Ameeruudin says her "craftsmanship is perfect and her language is simple, direct, lucid and lilting...with her facile, magical, eloquent and vibrating verses.

Always the free agent, Mary has never aligned herself with movements or groups, preferring to remain as uninfluenced by anything more as she is her own vision, and her muse as well as her own independently arrived at very positive philosophy.

She is the wife of artist, social activist & film-maker Richard E. Schiff. He has work in the Whitney Collection and The Museum of Fine Arts, Jerusalem, as well as many prominent collections around the world. He contributed to, and appears in, the Academy Award winning documentary "Freeheld." Mary is the daughter of artist Mary Sinclair and painter Will Barnet. She resides in a renovated barn, built in 1836, in New Jersey with her husband.

ABOUT RICHARD E. SCHIFF

 Richard E. Schiff is an American artist, born in Jersey City, NJ in 1947. His father Leonard W. Schiff was the son of world renowned musical singing star Fritzi Scheff and Jacob Schiff. Leonard was a well known miniaturist with work in the Metropolitan Museum of Art and The Helena Rubinstein Collection. His late mother Louise Mary Reier, was a writer.

Schiff began his studies at The Art Students League of New York in 1963, at 16 he was accepted in the adult painting class of Ernest Fiene, an artist called "the best working in America!" by Matisse on a visit to New York. Schiff also studied with Robert Beverly Hale, Jose DeCreeft, Will Barnet and Earl Mayan. Today, Schiff is a Life Member of the League.

In 1981 he created the first art curriculum in the Ocean County Vocational Technical School system and taught it to high school art majors for the first two years before returning to his own art work full time.

Schiff has been awarded a First Prize for Oil Painting by The American Association of University Women, and he has exhibited at Upsala University, Gallery 55 NYC, Avanti Gallery NYC, Center Art Gallery NYC, Gilford Gallery NYC, Dover Township Municipal Gallery NJ, Ocean Art Alliance NJ, Deal Center Gallery NJ, Kevin Cooper Galleries and Robert Baum Galleries NJ.

His work is in the Collection of the Whitney Family, The Gerard Family Collection, Bette Midler Collection, and the Museum of Fine Art, Jerusalem.

The drawings in this book represent a return to drawing from life begun in 2008 and continuing through the present. Schiff works from a renovated horse barn built in 1836, in South Jersey, with his wife Mary Barnet.